Hearst Castle

An American Palace

By Barbara Knox

Consultant: Stephen F. Brown, Director
Institute of Medieval Philosophy and Theology, Boston College

BEARPORT
PUBLISHING COMPANY, INC.

New York, New York

Credits

Cover, Victoria Garagliano/©Hearst Castle®/CA State Parks; title page, Victoria Garagliano/©Hearst Castle®/CA State Parks.

Background portrait throughout, Library of Congress Prints and Photographs Division; page 4, ©Hearst Castle®/CA State Parks; 5, Courtesy of the Bancroft Library, University of California, Berkeley, California; 6, Bettmann / CORBIS; 7, Ted Streshinsky/Hearst Castle/CA Park Service/CORBIS; 8(t), ©Hearst Castle®/CA State Parks; 8(b), Pawel Libera / CORBIS; 9, Courtesy of the Bancroft Library, University of California, Berkeley, California; 10(both), Nostalgiaville; 11, Library of Congress Prints and Photographs Division; 13, ©Hearst Castle®/CA State Parks; 14, 15, 16, 17(l), Victoria Garagliano/©Hearst Castle®/CA State Parks; 17(r), Zdravko Barov/©Hearst Castle®/CA State Parks; 18, David Sanger Photography / Alamy; 19, Bettmann / CORBIS; 20, Victoria Garagliano/©Hearst Castle®/CA State Parks; 21(t), Julia Morgan Collection, Special Collections, California Polytechnic State University; 21(b), ©Hearst Castle®/CA State Parks; 22, Victoria Garagliano/©Hearst Castle®/CA State Parks; 23, The Kobal Collection; 24, Library of Congress Prints and Photographs Division; 25, Bettmann / CORBIS; 26-27, Fred Lyon; 29, Victoria Garagliano/©Hearst Castle®/CA State Parks.

Original design and production by Dawn Beard Creative, Triesta Hall of Blu-Design, and Octavo Design and Production, Inc.

Library of Congress Cataloging-in-Publication Data

Knox, Barbara.
 Hearst Castle: an American palace / by Barbara Knox; consultant, Stephen F. Brown.
  p. cm.—(Castles, palaces & tombs)
 Includes bibliographical references and index.
 ISBN 1-59716-069-5 (library binding)—ISBN 1-59716-106-3 (pbk.)
 1. Hearst, William Randolph, 1863–1951—Juvenile literature. 2. Publishers and publishing—United States—Biography—Juvenile literature. 3. Hearst Castle (Calif.)—Juvenile literature.
 4. Castles—California—San Simeon—Juvenile literature. I. Brown, Stephen F. II. Title. III. Series.

 Z473.H4K59 2006
 070.5'092—dc22

                        2005005206

For more information, write to Bearport Publishing Company, Inc., 101 Fifth Avenue, Suite 6R, New York, New York 10003. Printed in the United States of America.

                    1 2 3 4 5 6 7 8 9 10

Table of Contents

A Night at Hearst Castle

Servants rushed through the castle, cleaning and making beds. Sewers were busy making costumes. Wigmakers hurried to finish the fancy wigs. Outside, 100 gardeners trimmed the lawns and clipped the flowers. William Randolph Hearst was having a party.

Hearst Castle at night

Soon the guests arrived. The Mayor of New York City flew in on a plane. Movie stars came in **limousines**. They filled the castle's 56 bedrooms. Laughing, they dressed in their costumes and put on their wigs. Then they all went downstairs to wish William a happy birthday. No one wanted to miss a minute of a party at Hearst Castle.

William (center) poses for a photo with some of his movie-star friends.

William once had a circus party where all the guests dressed as clowns, jugglers, and lion tamers. He even brought in a merry-go-round.

Millions of Dollars

William Hearst loved life. When he found something he enjoyed doing, he did it with all his heart.

William began his **career** running newspapers. Soon he began to **publish** magazines, too. Then he started radio and television companies. William also owned cattle ranches, silver mines, and castles in Europe. He was such a great businessman that U.S. presidents called him for advice.

William Randolph Hearst

William made millions of dollars. He also spent millions of dollars. He built a huge home near Los Angeles, California. He filled six warehouses with his art collection. William's most expensive project, however, was the castle he built in San Simeon, California.

This Bavarian-style home is on the grounds of William's estate, Wyntoon. It is located near Mount Shasta, California.

William's father was a U.S. Senator. In 1903, William was elected to the U.S. House of Representatives.

Two Ways of Life

William grew up around castles. When he was ten years old, he traveled on a huge ship to Europe. William and his mother visited castles in France, Germany, and England. When William saw Windsor Castle in England, he said, "I would like to live there."

William as a baby with his mother

Windsor Castle

As much as he liked castles, William also loved camping in the **wilderness**. His family owned a ranch called Camp Hill in California. There the family often set up tents and slept outdoors. William loved to race his pony through the rocky hills. As he grew older and traveled the world, William always came back to Camp Hill.

William often got into trouble for playing pranks when he was a boy. He once set off fireworks in his bedroom as an April Fool's joke.

Ready for Change

William began running his first newspaper when he was just 24 years old. He loved the work. Soon he began buying more newspapers. William's newspapers covered the news across the country and around the world.

In 1913, a copy of *Hearst's Magazine* cost 15 cents. Today many magazines cost about $3.99.

By 1918, William was 55 years old. He lived in a 30-room apartment in New York City with his wife and five sons. He owned 28 newspapers and 18 magazines. He had finished two terms in the U.S. House of Representatives. Now William was ready for a new project. He decided it was time to build a house at Camp Hill.

William ran for governor of New York in 1906, but lost the election.

Building Hearst Castle

William traveled to San Francisco to see **architect** Julia Morgan. He told her that he was tired of sleeping in tents at Camp Hill. He wanted to build a small house on his mountain.

Building a house on top of a mountain in 1919 was not easy. Workers worried about rattlesnake and **tarantula** bites. They worked long hours bringing building materials six miles (10 km) up a steep dirt road. When it rained, the road turned to mud. The trucks slipped and slid as they brought up the supplies.

ENGLAND

GERMANY

EUROPE

FRANCE

ATLANTIC OCEAN

ASIA

AFRICA

Workers began building Hearst Castle in September 1919. Work continued on the castle until 1947.

A Small Town

William kept adding to the plan for his "small house." First he wanted three large guesthouses. Then he decided he needed a huge outdoor swimming pool. Next came a zoo, an indoor pool, and a pool house with 17 dressing rooms.

Soon Hearst Castle became a small town. Workers lived in houses near the castle. Julia Morgan designed an office building for William. He could run his newspapers from the castle grounds.

The Roman Pool was the castle's indoor pool. It was built to look like an ancient Roman bath.

In the 1930s, Hearst Castle featured the largest private zoo in the world. The zoo included lions, tigers, polar bears, zebras, and monkeys.

Ancient Treasures

William wanted Hearst Castle to be perfect. Once he drove up the mountain to see the **construction**. On the way, he saw a guesthouse he didn't like. He told the workers to tear it down and rebuild it in another spot.

Hearst filled his study with expensive treasures from his travels.

William often traveled to Europe to find art and furniture for the castle. He bought ancient painted ceiling panels and huge marble fireplaces. He found carved wooden doors and golden **chandeliers**. Soon every room in the castle was filled with wonderful treasures.

Forty-one fireplaces can be found in Hearst Castle.

The oldest pieces of art at Hearst Castle are Greek vases. They are more than 2,700 years old.

Sitting Down to Dinner

William and his family moved into the castle on Christmas Day in 1925. William dressed up as Santa Claus. Each of his five sons had his own Christmas tree set up in the dining room.

The dining room during Christmas

The dining room soon became William's favorite place in the castle. The huge wooden table could seat 80 people. William sat in the middle of the table. His newest guest sat nearby so William could talk with him or her. Every night the guest would move down a seat. When a guest reached the end of the table, he or she knew it was time to go home!

William (center) entertaining his guests in the dining room

William always kept ketchup bottles and pickle jars on the table. He wanted everyone to remember that Hearst Castle was really just a ranch.

Time to Party

By the late 1920s, Hearst Castle was famous for its parties. Hollywood movie stars and **politicians** would arrive after dark. They found the castle glowing with light.

Neptune Pool took workers about 12 years to build. It's the largest outdoor heated swimming pool in the world.

In the morning, guests could walk through the gardens or play tennis. They fed the giraffes, camels, and **yaks** in the zoo. They went swimming in Neptune Pool. Guides led them into the mountains on long horseback rides.

After dinner the guests dressed up in colorful costumes. Everyone danced as the band played under the stars. At midnight fireworks lit up the sky.

Julia Morgan, who designed Hearst Castle, with a baby elephant in the zoo

Polar bears at Hearst's zoo

Entertaining the Guests

William loved going to the movies. He enjoyed them so much that he started a movie company called Cosmopolitan Productions. His company made some of the first movies in the 1920s.

Inside the castle's movie theater

William wanted to share his love of movies with his guests. So he added a theater to the castle. The theater seated 50 people. Every night he would show a movie twice, once for the servants and once for the guests. A big pile of fur coats was kept inside the theater. The guests snuggled up inside them while they watched the show.

Guests at Hearst Castle enjoy a movie

William also liked plays. When he went to see a play, he bought two seats, one for himself and one for his hat.

23

Never Finished

In 1939, the world was not at peace. When Germany, a country in Europe, attacked Poland, World War II began. William stopped construction on his castle until the war was over.

The castle as it looked around 1947

By 1947, however, William was growing tired. He was 84 years old. He decided it was time to stop adding on to the castle. Hearst Castle would never be completely finished.

William was 88 years old when he died in 1951. He left behind businesses and land worth more than $400 million. Six years after his death, his company, the Hearst Corporation, gave the castle to the State of California.

Many people came to Hearst's funeral, which took place in San Francisco, California.

All five of William's sons went into the newspaper business. William's grandson George heads the Hearst Corporation today.

Visiting Hearst Castle

Millions of people have visited Hearst Castle since it opened to the public in 1958. Many visitors drive along the California coast from Los Angeles. They stop in the small town of San Simeon. Then they take a bus up the mountain to see the castle.

Casa Del Monte
(a guesthouse)

Neptune Pool

Casa Del Sol
(a guesthouse)

Casa Del Mar
(a guesthouse)

Inside, silver lamps, rare paintings, and marble statues still fill the rooms. Visitors can see where William Hearst slept. If they peek out the window, they might spot a zebra grazing on the hill. Even though it was never finished, Hearst Castle remains one of the greatest homes ever built in America.

Roman Pool

Casa Grande (main house)

Visitors can take a special night tour of Hearst Castle. Guides dress in 1930s clothes. They show what it was like to live at the castle during William Hearst's time.

Just the Facts

- William Randolph Hearst's father owned **stock** in the Comstock Lode, one of the richest silver mines in the United States.

- William's first job was as a **reporter**. He worked for the *World* newspaper in New York.

- William named his castle "The Enchanted Hill." Many people call the castle "San Simeon" after the nearby town. Today, the buildings are most often called "Hearst Castle."

- There are 38 bedrooms and 41 bathrooms in the main house at Hearst Castle. The three guesthouses have another 18 bedrooms and 20 bathrooms.

- The Roman Pool, which is indoors, is covered with thousands of real gold and glass tiles. It cost more than $1 million to build in 1934.

- In 1941, Orson Welles made a movie called *Citizen Kane*. The movie is based on the life of William Randolph Hearst. Many people believe *Citizen Kane* is one of the greatest movies ever made.

Timeline

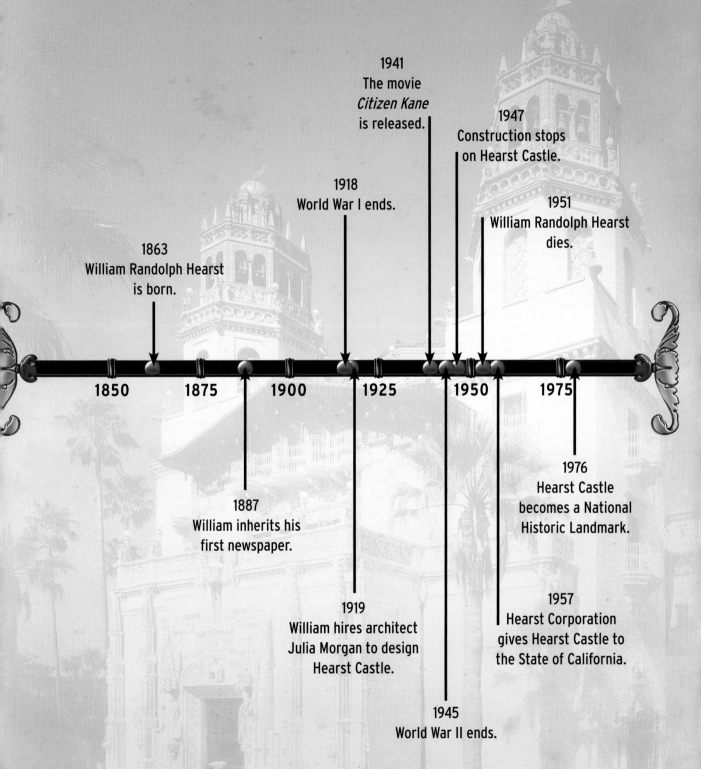

1941
The movie
Citizen Kane
is released.

1947
Construction stops
on Hearst Castle.

1918
World War I ends.

1951
William Randolph Hearst
dies.

1863
William Randolph Hearst
is born.

1887
William inherits his
first newspaper.

1850   1875   1900   1925   1950   1975

1919
William hires architect
Julia Morgan to design
Hearst Castle.

1976
Hearst Castle
becomes a National
Historic Landmark.

1957
Hearst Corporation
gives Hearst Castle to
the State of California.

1945
World War II ends.

Glossary

architect (AR-ki-tekt) a person who designs buildings and manages their construction

career (kuh-RIHR) a lifelong job

chandeliers (*shan*-duh-LIHRZ) decorative hanging lights

construction (kuhn-STRUHKT-shuhn) the building of something such as a house or bridge

limousines (*lim*-uh-ZEENS) long, expensive cars that have glass dividers between the driver and the passengers

politicians (pol-uh-TISH-uhnz) people who are members of a branch of government

publish (PUHB-lish) to produce printed material such as newspapers, magazines, or books

reporter (ri-POR-tur) somebody whose job is to find out facts and tell other people about them

stock (STOK) the part of a company that a person owns after he or she invests money in it

tarantula (tuh-RAN-chuh-luh) a large spider with a hairy body and legs

wilderness (WIL-dur-niss) a natural place such as a forest or mountain where few people live

yaks (YAKS) large oxen with long hair and long curved horns that come from Tibet, a region in central Asia

Bibliography

Coffman, Taylor. *Hearst Castle: The Story of William Randolph Hearst and San Simeon.* Santa Barbara, CA: ARA Leisure Services (1985).

Frazier, Nancy. *William Randolph Hearst.* Englewood Cliffs, NJ: Silver Burdett Press (1989).

Kastner, Victoria. *Hearst Castle: The Biography of a Country House.* New York: Harry N. Abrams, Inc. (2000).

Murray, Ken. *The Golden Days of San Simeon.* Garden City, NY: Doubleday & Co., Inc. (1971).

Read More

Hindley, Judy. *Knights & Castles.* Tulsa, OK: EDC Publishing (2003).

Jeunesse, Gallimard. *Castles: A First Discovery Book.* New York: Scholastic (1990).

Osborne, Will, and Mary Pope Osborne. *Knights and Castles: Magic Tree House Research Guide.* New York: Random House (2000).

Learn More Online

Visit these Web sites to learn more about Hearst Castle:

architecture.about.com/library/blhearst-morgan.htm

www.bluffton.edu/~sullivanm/jmhearstss/intro.html

www.hearstcastle.org/welcome.asp

Index

About the Author

Barbara Knox has written about Dracula's Castle in Romania
and the Forbidden City in China.
She loves visiting castles.